Contents

Page

Sea Change at Viking Point

Chapter 1 The Oflight Inspection

Kez groaned. She was trapped. "I'll never get past Level Seven," she muttered, turning to look out of the window. The fog had been wrapped around the house for days. She groaned again as the foghorn boomed out its warning.

"You have email," said a cheerful voice. Kez tapped a key.

"Dad," she called, "there's a message for you."

Dad reached over and opened the email and then sighed. "Well, that's going to mean a lot of work," he said.

"What's that?" asked Kez's mum, peering over his shoulder at the screen.

"We're being inspected. Just listen to what they want us to do to prepare."

Dear Mr Portland, he read,

We are writing to inform you that an Office for Lighthouse Management (Oflight) team will be visiting you within the next two months in order to inspect your operation. In order to prepare for this visit, you will need to do the following:

1. *Complete and send documents X2147a, X2147b, SK 169 and GM 082 to the Oflight office.*
2. *Check that all signalling apparatus is in good working order.*
3. *Ascertain that standby equipment is fully operational.*

4. *Ensure that rescue resources, including life jackets, belts and flares, are in a state of readiness.*
5. *Survey the fabric of the building and prepare a written report on the same.*
6. *Review personal requirements, e.g. frequency and mode of communication with the mainland.*
7. *Inform our office of a suitable date for the visit.*
8. *Send details of the most appropriate means of travelling to and from the property known as Viking Point Lighthouse. Please include information about any personal effects the team might need to bring with them.*

"Well, we knew it would happen sooner or later," Mum said. "It's a shame Kris isn't here to help us get ready. Still, being part of the whale survey team is probably far more exciting than preparing for an inspection."

"I can do something," Kez said, eager to break the monotony of the last week.

"Get the tide tables then," Dad suggested, "and help me work out when they can come. The sooner they come, the sooner we'll get rid of them."

"Why don't you want them to come?" Kez asked.

"Oh it's just that they might think I'm not doing a good enough job and that could be the end of it."

"You're the best lighthouse keeper, Dad," Kez said.

"Oh yes? How many others do you know?" Dad teased.

Chapter 2 A Letter from Kris

The weeks leading up to the inspection passed quickly as the family cleaned and polished every inch of the lighthouse that had been their home for the whole of Kez's life. On the morning of the inspection Kez stood on the observation platform.

"I can see the boat," she called. "They're on their way."

The inspectors were with them for two days. Kez thought they seemed quite happy with the lighthouse and that Dad had nothing to worry about. In fact they seemed very impressed with Dad's maintenance of the old switching system.

The boat that came to pick the inspectors up also brought the weekly post. "There's a letter from Kris for you," Mum said, handing an envelope to Kez.

Kez hopped onto her bunk. Kris usually sent really interesting letters about his adventures with the survey team.

Somewhere in the Atlantic
3rd August

Hi Kez,

How did the inspection go? Tell me all about it when you write back. I've had an incredible couple of weeks out here. We left the Falkland Islands just over two weeks ago and set sail for the Antarctic. I just can't believe the scenery. There are hundreds of icebergs and some of them are enormous. On the very first day we were joined by flocks of seabirds, birds that we never see on Viking Point. We saw Wandering Albatross and Storm Petrels. Then, within a couple of days, we saw our first whales - which is, as I keep reminding myself, why we're here. They are so amazing.

I've enclosed a copy of an article I've had published in the Whale and Dolphin Conservation Society magazine. I thought you'd like to see my name in print!

Yesterday, we landed on Paulet Island which was covered with Adelie Penguins. The noise was tremendous.

As we've come further south, the days have lasted longer and longer. It's only dark for a couple of hours now which does make it hard to sleep.

Anyway, I'm due on watch now so I'll have to go.

Write back soon.

Take care.

Love, Kris.

Chapter 3 Mermaids and Orcas

Kez unfolded the magazine article that Kris had tucked into the envelope. She read the title, *Killer Whales by Kris Portland.* It made him sound very grown up. Rather to her surprise, she found the article very interesting, but her reply to him wouldn't be. She could only tell him about the inspection. There were no penguins, whales or even Storm Petrels to spot from Viking Point. She lay back on her bed, trying to come up with some ideas.

"Kez! Quick come up here!" Dad's excited voice broke into her thoughts. She ran up the stairs to where Dad was standing on the observation platform.

"What is it?" she asked. He pointed out to sea.

"Look, follow the line of my finger."

At first, Kez couldn't see what he was pointing at. Then, several dark shapes arced gracefully through the waves.

"Dolphins," Kez breathed.

As they watched, Dad told her about the creatures.

"In olden times, sailors thought that they were mermaids," he said.

Kez continue to watch the dolphins, intrigued by how they really did look like mermaids, with their tails dipping effortlessly into the sea.

Gradually, the dolphins disappeared from view.

Kez smiled at Dad. "I've just thought of something I can write an article about. I'll send it to Kris 'cos I bet he doesn't know anything about these creatures. I'm going to write about mermaids!"

Chapter 4 A Secluded Retreat

"Listen to this Bill," Mum said waving the latest copy of *Lighthouse Keepers' Monthly*. Dad looked up from the newspaper he was reading.

"*Wanted, secluded retreat for writer. Must have peace, quiet and no distractions*," she read. "We could offer all of that here."

"Peace, quiet and no distractions?" Dad asked as Kez bounced into the room. "I don't think so."

"Well, I think now that Kris's room is empty we should advertise it for short holidays. People think staying in a lighthouse is a great adventure. Don't you remember the Nashes told us they'd had guests?"

"I think it's a great idea, Mum," Kez said. "It's nice having people here. I liked it when the inspectors stayed."

Dad grunted and went back to his paper. Mum looked at Kez and said, "Let's write an advert. We'll make a list of all the good things about Viking Point."

Why does Dad question Mum's idea of "peace, quiet and no distractions"?

Chapter 5 Bad News

Kez was looking forward to the next post delivery. She thought there might be a letter from Kris and she wondered what he thought about her mermaid article. But when the post finally came it brought bad news. Dad sorted through the envelopes and packages.

"Ah. Here's one from Oflight. It'll be the result of our inspection." He opened the envelope and Kez could tell from his face that there was something wrong.

"What is it, Dad? Didn't they think we were doing a good job?"

"No. We were doing a great job. But they've decided to automate Viking Point."

"Read it to us, Bill," Mum said.

Dear Mr Portland,
Thank you for your hospitality during our recent visit. We were very impressed with the effort that you, and your family, put into the running and maintenance of Viking Point lighthouse.

However, the lighthouse upgrade programme that is currently being implemented means that within the next six months Viking Point will become fully automated. As a result, a resident lighthouse keeper will not be required.

If you wish to discuss this development with us, please do not hesitate to contact the office.

The family looked at each other.

"What will we do? Where will we live? On the mainland?" Kez asked.

Mum shook her head. "Oh no! They don't get rid of the Portlands that easily. We'll persuade them otherwise, just you see."

What do you think will happen next?

What sort of a person is Kez? Why do you think so?

KILLER WHALES

by Kris Portland

Orcinas orca, or killer whale, is a very large marine animal and can be found in all oceans of the world.

All killer whales have a streamlined hairless body, a horizontal tail fin and a blowhole for breathing on top of the head. They weigh between 4 and 10 tonnes and can measure up to 7 metres.

Orcas live in family groups called pods. The pods travel and hunt together. A female usually bears one calf every three to ten years. The pregnancy lasts for seventeen months. The calf is born tail first with its eyes open and measures almost three metres. As soon as it is born, the calf swims to the underside of its mother and starts feeding. The mother feeds her calf for about a year. The offspring often stay close to their mother for up to ten years.

Orcas need about fifty kilos of food a day so they spend a great deal of their time foraging. They feed on fish and other marine mammals. Orcas have been known to eat birds, sharks, squid and porpoise. They use their teeth to grasp and tear, not to chew. Most prey is swallowed whole. Some killer whales' stomachs have been found to contain entire seal carcasses.

When orcas are not hunting for food, their time is spent resting, travelling and playing. Play includes *porpoising* – swimming underwater and on the surface like a dolphin, *flipper slapping* – slapping the water with their tails and fins and *breeching* – the whale shoots straight up into the air and then falls down onto its belly, side or back. Orcas communicate with each other using echo-location and vocalisation. When orcas navigate or search for food, they echo-locate by sending out a stream of clicks and pulses. When they vocalise, they use whistles, squeaks, high and low tones which the other whales in the pod can recognise.

Despite their name, killer whales are on the whole friendly and non-aggressive towards humans. There is no record of anyone even being nibbled. In the past, many societies have associated them with good luck, strength and wisdom.

from the Whale and Dolphin Conservation Society Magazine

Creels – for all your fishing needs

We stock the latest models of Sawtooth rods and have a huge selection of floats

Just in – the new and improved Keepit keep nets

info@fishingline.net

Heat4feet

The latest space age technology is used in our novel foot warmers.

No more cold feet – guaranteed to stay warm overnight

To place an advertisement in these pages, please contact: The Sales Department, Lighthouse Keepers' Monthly, Cape Wrath.

Draught excluder

3 rolls for the price of 2

Contact: Mr J Grinling PO Box 723

Stir Crazy?!

The latest recipes for lighthouse bound cooks

50 different ways of cooking fish

½ price introductory offer – only £6.99

Buy 2 copies and get a free fish steamer

Finesterre Publishing Co. FI2 6KJ

Pirate ship bunks

Just the job for the smaller mem-bers of the crew

Fully rigged small scale schooner with cosy swaying hammock

Ample storage space for piratical equipment and other necessities

Captain Hook bedding also avail-able

Hand made by our craftsmen

Worried about your weight?

Longing for litheness?

Staggering up the stairs?

What you need is a Scampette!

Our unique and innovative exercise system

15 minutes a day on our combined trampette and exercise bike and you'll soon be in tip top condition.

Send now for a free no obligation one month trial.

Helicopter delivery can be arranged.

An Exciting Discovery

Fitness addict Denise Fisher got more than she bargained for during her daily jog along the beach at Eastcliffe Bay last Thursday. "I was just warming down near the rock pools when this disgusting smell hit me," she explained to our roving reporter. Then Denise found the source of the smell. It was like nothing she'd ever seen before.

"It was big – easily the size of a child. It was lying half in and half out of a rock pool. Its mouth was open and I could see a lot of very sharp teeth. And it had spines along its back. It was a dull browny colour and a bit mottled. And it stank!"

Denise attracted the attention of local angler Ken Stagnall who was fishing nearby and asked him what he thought the creature was. Ken was at a loss, so he took a photo of it on his mobile phone and sent it to a friend who works at the Marine Centre. His friend quickly alerted the authorities when he saw the photo. He felt that the creature looked very much like a Mareocanth, a species long thought to have been extinct.

Scientists have since confirmed this identification and the remains of the Mareocanth have been taken to the National Marine Museum for further investigation.

Ms Fisher said that she was thrilled when she heard that the scientists had nicknamed the creature *Denise* and that she would be following the story closely.

Denise Fisher who found the suspected Mareocanth, which has been dubbed 'Denise' in her honour.

WANTED

Have you seen this fish?

BEWARE! DO NOT TOUCH!

It is thought that the Mareocanth's skin contains a poisonous irritant.

What the Experts Say

Experts are intrigued by the recent discovery of a Mareocanth on our beaches. Professor Phinn of the National Marine Museum has this explanation to offer. "This is a very significant discovery, as scientists have long believed this fish to be extinct. It now appears that this is not the case. The world is aware, from recent tragic events, that there has been an upsurge in deep sea volcanic activity. It may be that this has disturbed a Mareocanth colony and caused them to disperse. We assume that they live at a very great depth in the ocean and strong currents may also have swept them from their usual habitat.

The particular Mareocanth *Denise* that was found here showed no sign of injury or damage, so how it found its way onto the beach is unclear.

Professor Phinn

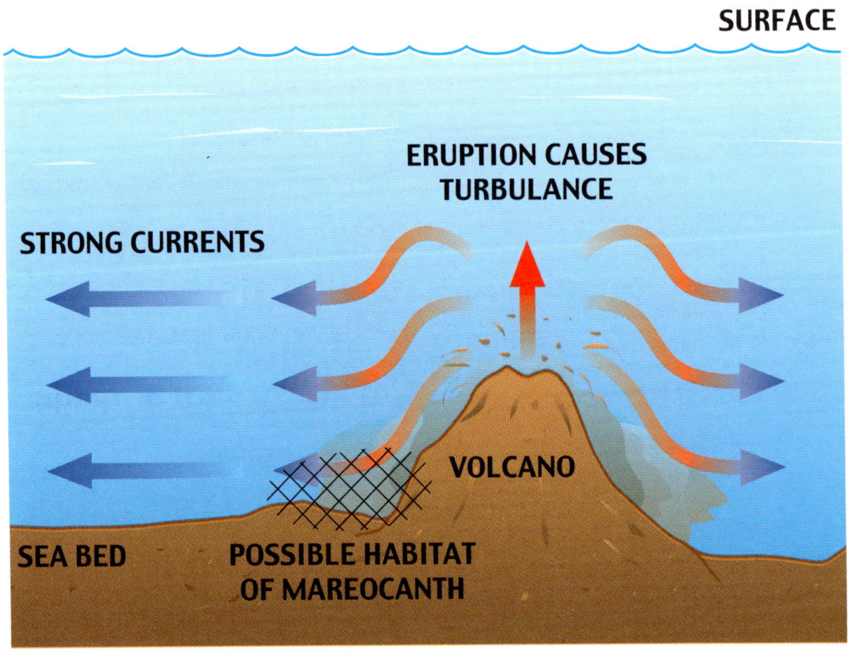

Perhaps it was weakened by the turbulent nature of the seas. This would have meant that it could not resist the tidal pull and as a result it was beached. Obviously, no fish can live for long when removed from its normal environment.

It is possible that as we examine the creature further, other evidence will be revealed, and as it is we will post our findings on the NMM website." Lighthouse keepers and their families in particular are asked to keep a weather eye out for any further sightings of this fascinating survival from pre-history.

Announcement

Scientists from the National Marine Museum have asked lighthouse keepers particularly to be on the alert. They have issued the following guidance for what to do if you think you have found a Mareocanth.

- Do not touch the creature.
- If it is out of water, ensure that the skin is kept moist. Splash or spray with seawater. Do not use fresh or warm water as this will cause skin damage.
- Keep children and animals away.
- Contact the National Marine Museum and inform them of the position and condition of the creature.

We are Not Amused

Contents

SIREN SONG

1 AUGUST 1981

Dear Tape Recorder,

This is me. My name's Roger and I'm nine years old today. You're my birthday present.

Happy birthday to me,
Happy birthday to you,
Happy birthday, dear both of us...

1 AUGUST 1982

R for Roger. R for Roger. This is Roger, mark ten, calling. I'm not going to bore you with a bite-by-bite account of my birthday tea, like last year. This time I'll only record the exciting moments in my life. Over and out.

1 AUGUST 1983

My name is Roger Kent. I am eleven years old. I want to get this down in case anything happens to me.

I hate this village. I wish we hadn't come to live here. There's something funny about it.

For one thing, there are no other children here. Except Billy Watson, and he's weird.

He's a thin, white-faced boy who jumps when you speak to him. Mum says he's been ill, and I must be kind. I was. I asked him to come to my birthday tea today. He twitched like I'd stabbed him in the back, and his eyes scuttled about like beetles. Then he mumbled something and ran off.

The grown-ups are peculiar, too. They're old and baggy-eyed, as if they'd been crying all night. When they see me, they stop talking. They watch me. It's a bit scary.

At first I thought they didn't like me. But it's not that. They look as if they know something terrible's going to happen to me, and are sorry about it.

Mrs Mason's the worst. I hate the way she looks at me. Her eyes are ... I dunno ... sort of hungry. I don't mean she's a cannibal. It's more like ... D'you know why gerbils sometimes eat their own babies? It's because they're afraid they're in danger, and think they'll be safer back inside.

That's just how Mrs Mason looks at me. As if she'd like to swallow me to keep me safe. But what from?

This morning, when she heard it was my birthday, she hugged me. I jerked away. I didn't mean to be rude. I honestly thought she was going to start nibbling my ear. That's the sort of state I'm in.

"Never go out at night," she said. (That's nothing, Mum's always telling me that nowadays. It's what came next.) "Never go out at night, *whatever sounds you hear!*"

Funny thing to say, wasn't it? "Whatever sounds you hear."

I've been thinking and thinking, but I can't imagine what she meant. If we lived by the sea, I'd think of smugglers. You know, like that poem – *Watch the wall, my darling, while the gentlemen go by…*

Why does Roger say Mrs Mason looks at him "sort of hungry?"

Perhaps they're witches! I'm not being silly. There *are* witches nowadays. It was in the papers once. COVEN OF WITCHED EXPOSED, it said. They certainly were exposed! There was this photograph of men and women with nothing on. Not that you could see much, only their backs. They didn't look wild and exciting at all. Just stupid. And cold – you could almost see the goose pimples. Still, they were witches.

D'you think it's that?

Full moon tonight. I'm going to stay awake and listen. It must be happening somewhere near enough for me to hear, or she wouldn't have said that.

Supposing they use our garden?

Suppose Mum's joined them! She's a bit strange lately. No that's silly.

10.30pm. I'm sitting by the window. Nothing's happened yet. Just the usual night noises, and not many of those. This village dies after ten o'clock. A dog barking. An owl getting on my nerves, can't the stupid thing say anything else?

It's boring. I think I'll go to bed for a bit.

0.00. I've got a digital clock and that's what it says. Like Time's laid eggs in a row. No time. Nothing point nothing nothing time. Don't count your minutes before they're hatched.

What's that?

Only an owl. The window's wide open, and it's cold. The moon is round and bright. There are shadows all over the garden. I can't see anything. It's very quiet now. No wind.

Listen!

Children! I can hear children laughing. I can hear their voices calling softly ...

I think they're in Billy Watson's garden. He must be having a midnight party, and he hasn't asked me! Pig! No wonder he ran off when I invited him to tea.

I wish I could see them. There're too many trees. Too many shadows.

Listen!

This microphone's too small. I held it out of the window, but I didn't get anything.

They were singing. Their voices were high and clear. I could hear every word. It was a funny little tune. Sort of sad, but nice. There's a chorus where they all hoot softly like baby owls. I think I can remember the words –

Little ghost, all dressed in white,
Walking on a summer's night,
(Hoooo, hooo,)
Calling to her childhood friend,
Asking him to come and play,
But his hair stands up on end.
Billy Watson runs away.

Billy Watson! So they *are* friends of his! I suppose they're playing a game ...

Listen...

What does Billy Watson know that Roger doesn't know?

It was a girl singing alone this time. I'm sure it was a girl. Her voice was so high and sweet and sad, it made me ache. This is what she sang –

Don't you love me any more?
I'm as pretty as before.
(Hooo, hoo,)
Though my roses all are gone,
Lily-white is just as sweet.
Stars shine through me now, not on
Flesh that's only so much meat.

I wish I could see her....

"*Coo-ee!* Over here!"

They heard me. I know they did. They're whispering. Now they're coming nearer. I can hear the bushes rustling by our wall. Look! I think one of them's slipped over into our garden. It's difficult to be sure. There are so many shadows. I'm going to dangle the microphone out of the window ...

Listen!

Billy, see the moon is bright.
Won't you play with me tonight?
(Hooo, hoo,)
Billy Watson's now in bed,
With fingers in his ears,
And his blankets hide his head,
And his face is wet with tears.

I got it that time! It's very faint, but you can just make out the words. I don't think they can be friends of Billy's after all. They sounded as if they were mocking him. I wonder who they are?

Oh, they're going away now! I can hear them running through the bushes. Laughing. They've gone!

Is the microphone really too small to pick up the children's singing?

No. There's still one standing in the shadow of the lilac tree. Just below my window. I'm sure it's the girl. I can see her white frock gleaming ... unless it's just moonlight. She's all alone now. Waiting for me.

Listen!

Little ghost all dressed in white
Singing sadly in the night,
(Hooo, hooo,)
Who will play with me instead?
Must I be lonely till the end?
Is there any child abed
Brave enough to be my friend?

I'm coming! Wait for me! I know I promised Mum I'd never go out at night, but ... The moon is shining bright as day. Someone is singing in the garden below. Softly. Sweetly. Surely it won't matter if I go out just once?

The rest of the tape is blank. Roger Kent was never seen again.

Vivien Alcock

Could there be another explanation?

The Last Train Ride – 1879

Everyone was in a hurry to get home – Scotsmen returning to Scotland for the holidays, families who had been south for Christmas, workers anxious to get back to the warmth of a fireside and a good supper … Though Christmas was over, the New Year was still to come.

It was a filthy night, but the lights of Dundee burned all the brighter for that. And crossing over the Tay would be part of the fun. The new bridge was still a wonder to those contemplating a trip over it – a stone and metal monument to progress and prosperity.

By seven in the evening, the wind was howling, hurling itself against the signal boxes as if it would swallow them whole; unfurling dense, silver banners of rain across the starless sky. With each new gust, the carriages juddered and the luggage jumped about in the luggage van. Children with their noses pressed to the steamy windows would recoil against their mothers, then be drawn back to cloud the windows even more with their excited breathing. The noisy rhythm of the wheels on the track – "nearly-there-nearly-there-nearly-there" – was all but drowned by the storm.

What was the train ride like before the accident? How can you tell?

Then, all of a sudden, the countryside of lashing trees and huddled buildings gave way to rainy darkness: the train was crossing the Firth of Tay (though the river far below was not even visible through the rain). The locomotive gave a baleful whistle which the wind tore in shreds.

Two signalmen stood discussing the safety of their signal box – whether it might blow down, whether the storm would blow itself out by morning or racket on into Hogmanay. The London–Dundee train went by them wrapped in its cloak of sooty steam, slowing down for the bridge. Out over the Tay it thundered, a snake of lights, a wisp of white steam. Then a plume of sparks rose up – golden rain amid the silver. There was a tremendous flash.

Too far off for sound to carry. But as the signalmen watched, the snake of lighted carriages disappeared abruptly from sight.

Passengers on board, tumbled together by sudden braking, felt nothing now – nothing but an absence of sound. Oddly, for a second or two, the rain outside the windows rained upwards, because they were falling so fast. No time for anything more than a joining of hands, then the Tay was boiling over the wreckage and the storm was hooting.

Why was the new bridge a wonder for the people?

Running down to the foreshore, the two signalmen shouted out at every tight-closed front door they passed: "*The bridge! The bridge! The train!*" But when they reached the mudflats (where the waves were breaking big as the open sea) there was nothing to do but stare into blackness. With a triumphant flourish, the storm uncovered the moon, briefly casting a ghastly, ghostly pallor over the river. The whole centre section of the Tay Bridge was gone, like a smile with its teeth smashed away. The train must have driven out on to thin air, then plunged into the deep, icy water of the Tay.

Next day, divers were needed to find the sunken train, rolled and scoured by the river's current. Of the seventy-nine people aboard, not one lived to see in the New Year of 1880.

How long did it take the train to fall into the river? How do we know?

Article from *The Times* 29 Dec 1879 on Tay Bridge Crash

DREADFUL ACCIDENT ON THE TAY BRIDGE

LOSS OF PASSENGER TRAIN

Dundee, Sunday midnight

To-night a heavy gale swept over Dundee and a portion of the Tay Bridge was blown down while a train from Edinburgh due at 7.15 was passing. It is believed that the train is in the water, but the gale is still so strong that a steamboat has not yet been able to reach the bridge. The train was duly signalled from Fife as having entered the bridge at 7.14. It was seen running along the rails, and then suddenly was observed a flash of fire. The opinion was that the train left the rails, and went over the bridge. Those who saw the incident repaired immediately to the Tay-bridge station at Dundee and informed the station master of what they had seen. He immediately put himself in communication with the

man in charge of the signal-box at the north end of the bridge. The telegraph wires are stretched across the bridge, but when the instrument was tried it was soon seen that the wires were broken.

Mr. Smith, the station-master and Mr. Roberts, locomotive superintendent, determined, notwithstanding the fierce gale, to walk across the bridge as far as possible from the north side, with the view of ascertaining the extent of the disaster. They were able to get out a considerable distance, and the first thing that caught their eye was the water spurting from a pipe which was laid across the bridge for the supply of Newport, a village on the south side, from the Dundee reservoirs. Going a little further, they could distinctly see by the aid of the strong moonlight that there was a large gap in the bridge caused by the fall, so far as they could discern, of two or three of the largest spars. They thought, however, that they observed a red light on the south part of the bridge, and were of the opinion that the train had been brought to a standstill on the driver noticing the accident. This conjecture has, unfortunately, been proved incorrect. At Broughtyferry, four miles from the bridge, several mail bags have come ashore, and there is no doubt that the train is in the river. No precise information as to the number of passengers can be obtained, but it is variously estimated at from 150 to 200.

The Provost and a number of leading citizens of Dundee started at half-past 10 o'clock in a steam-boat for the bridge, the gale being moderated; but they have not yet returned.

Monday, 1.30 a.m.
The scene at the Tay-bridge station to-night is simply appalling. Many thousand persons are congregated around the buildings, and strong men and women are wringing their hands in despair. On the 2nd of October 1877, while the bridge was in course of construction, one of the girders was blown down during a gale similar to that of to-day, but only one of the workmen lost his life. The return of the steamboat is anxiously awaited.

The Times, 29th December 1879

What early evidence was there that part of the bridge had been destroyed?

What evidence was there that the train had fallen into the river?

Life of Charles Dickens

1812 Born on Friday 7th February in Portsmouth

1814 Family move to London

1821 Father loses his job

1824 Father arrested for debt and sent to prison. Charles starts work in blacking factory. Father later released

1827 Charles leaves school, becomes office boy, decides to become reporter

1831 Charles is a parliamentary reporter

1836 Marries Catherine Hogarth. First part of Pickwick Papers published

1837 Begins *Oliver Twist*. Catherine has the first of their 10 children – a son, Charles

1842 Travels through Canada and the USA

1843 *A Christmas Carol* is published

1845 Starts amateur theatrical company

1848 Directs and acts in amateur theatricals

1856 Buys Gad's Hill – a large house in London that he has always liked

1857 His theatre company performs for Queen Victoria. Charles falls in love with Ellen Ternan, an actress

1858 In London, performs his first paid readings. Separates from his wife

1863 Performs readings in Paris

1865 Charles and Ellen involved in serious rail crash

1867 Performs readings in USA, despite doctors' advice

1868 Dies on June 9th. Buried on June 14th

Table Rules for Little Folks

around 1858

In silence I must take my seat,
And give God thanks before I eat;
Must for my food in patience wait,
Till I am asked to hand my plate;
I must not scold, nor whine, nor pout,
Nor move my chair nor plate about;
With knife, or fork, or napkin ring,
I must not play, nor must I sing.
I must not speak a useless word,
For children should be seen, not heard;
I must not talk about my food,
Nor fret if I don't think it good;
I must not say, "The bread is old,"
"The tea is hot," "The coffee's cold";
My mouth with food I must not crowd,
Nor while I'm eating speak aloud;
Must turn my head to cough or sneeze,
And when I ask, say "If you please";
The tablecloth I must not spoil,
Nor with my food my fingers soil;
Must keep my seat when I have done,
Nor round the table sport or run;
When told to rise, then I must put
My chair away with noiseless foot;
And lift my heart to God above,
In praise for all his wondrous love.

THE CHATTERBOX.

Why do you think the writer feels these rules were needed?

Why do you think the rules are in verse form?

Good and Bad Children

Children, you are very little,
And your bones are very brittle;
If you would grow great and stately,
You must try to walk sedately.

You must still be bright and quiet,
And content with simple diet;
And remain, through all bewild'ring,
Innocent and honest children.

Happy hearts and happy faces,
Happy play in grassy places –
That was how, in ancient ages,
Children grew to kings and sages.

But the unkind and the unruly,
And the sort who eat unduly,
They must never hope for glory –
Theirs is quite a different story!

Cruel children, crying babies,
All grow up as geese and gabies,
Hated, as their age increases,
By their nephews and their nieces.

Robert Louis Stevenson

A Farewell

My fairest child, I have no song to give you;
No lark could pipe to skies so dull and grey:
Yet, ere we part, one lesson I can leave you
For every day.

Be good, sweet maid, and let who will be clever;
Do noble things, not dream them, all day long;
And so make life, death, and that vast forever
One grand, sweet song.

Charles Kingsley

What do you think we are being told in these poems?
Are there any words you don't understand? Can you work them out?

Summary of *A Christmas Carol*

Ebenezer Scrooge is the world's biggest miser. He's mean, grasping and cold. He pays his clerk, Bob Cratchit, a measly salary and will only allow him a very small fire. Scrooge's only family, a nephew named Fred, tries to persuade him to spend Christmas at his house. Scrooge's only reply is "Bah! Humbug!"

On Christmas Eve, Scrooge is visited by the ghost of his former work partner, Jacob Marley. Marley tells Scrooge that this is his last hope of changing his miserly ways. He will be visited by three ghosts – the Ghost of Christmas Past, the Ghost of Christmas Present and the Ghost of Christmas Yet to Come. Scrooge dismisses Marley, saying "there's more of gravy than of grave about you, whatever you are" and goes to sleep.

The Ghost of Christmas Past takes Scrooge back to see himself as a young boy, alone in a school at Christmas. They visit a later Christmas where Scrooge watches in horror as he sees himself break off the engagement between himself and his fiancée Belle. Scrooge is also shown happier times, as he sees himself apprenticed to the kind and merry merchant Fezzywig. He starts to realise that he doesn't treat his own clerk in the same way.

The Ghost of Christmas Present takes Scrooge to Bob Cratchit's house. It is Cratchit's one day off in the year and although the family are extremely poor, they make every effort to enjoy themselves. Even Tiny Tim, their crippled son, makes a brave attempt to have fun. Scrooge is worried about Tim and asks if he will live. The Ghost says that, in the future, he can see an empty seat and a crutch without an owner. Scrooge begs for Tim to be spared. Next he is taken to Fred's house, to the party he had refused to go to. He sees the family having great fun and is very surprised when they drink a toast to their Uncle Scrooge.

The Ghost of Christmas Yet to Come is terrifying, dark and silent. He shows Scrooge that he will have no one to grieve for him when he dies and that his only maidservant will steal from him.

The following morning, Scrooge wakes up and is thrilled to find that it is still Christmas. He starts to make amends for his miserliness. He sends a turkey anonymously to Cratchit's family. Then, much to everyone's surprise, he goes to dinner at Fred's where he has the best Christmas ever. He proves he has had a complete change of heart by giving Bob Cratchit a pay rise and is so good to his family that he becomes like a second father to Tim. Tiny Tim has the last word: "God bless us, every one!"

"A Merry Christmas to You"

"I don't know what to do," cried Scrooge, laughing and crying in the same breath; and making a perfect Laocöon of himself with his stockings. "I am as light as a feather, I am as happy as an angel, I am as merry as a schoolboy. I am as giddy as a drunken man. A merry Christmas to everybody. A happy New Year to all the world. Hallo here. Whoop. Hallo."

He had frisked into the sitting-room, and was now standing there: perfectly winded.

"There's the saucepan that the gruel was in," cried Scrooge, starting off again, and frisking round the fireplace. "There's the door, by which the Ghost of Jacob Marley entered. There's the corner where the Ghost of Christmas Present, sat. There's the window where I saw the wandering Spirits. It's all right, it's all true, it all happened. Ha ha ha."

Really, for a man who had been out of practice for so many years, it was a splendid laugh, a most illustrious laugh. The father of a long, long line of brilliant laughs.

"I don't know what day of the month it is," said Scrooge. "I don't know how long I've been among the Spirits. I don't know anything. I'm quite a baby. Never mind. I don't care. I'd rather be a baby. Hallo. Whoop. Hallo here."

He was checked in his transports by the churches ringing out the lustiest peals he had ever heard. Clash, clang, hammer; ding, dong, bell. Bell, dong, ding; hammer, clang, clash. Oh, glorious, glorious.

Running to the window, he opened it, and put out his head. No fog, no mist; clear, bright, jovial, stirring, cold; cold, piping for the blood to dance to; golden sunlight; heavenly sky; sweet fresh air; merry bells. Oh, glorious. Glorious!

"What's to-day?" cried Scrooge, calling downward to a boy in Sunday clothes, who perhaps had loitered to look about him.

"EH?" returned the boy, with all his might of wonder.

"What's to-day, my fine fellow?" said Scrooge.

"To-day!" replied the boy. "Why, CHRISTMAS DAY."

"It's Christmas Day!" said Scrooge to himself. "I haven't missed it. The Spirits have done it all in one night. They can do anything they like. Of course they can. Of course they can. Hallo, my fine fellow!"

"Hallo!" returned the boy.

"Do you know the Poulterer's, in the next street but one, at the corner?" Scrooge inquired.

"I should hope I did," replied the lad.

"An intelligent boy!" said Scrooge. "A remarkable boy! Do you know whether they've sold the prize Turkey that was hanging up there? Not the little prize Turkey: the big one?"

"What, the one as big as me?" returned the boy.

"What a delightful boy!" said Scrooge. "It's a pleasure to talk to him. Yes, my buck!"

"It's hanging there now," replied the boy.

"Is it?" said Scrooge. "Go and buy it."

"Walk-ER!" exclaimed the boy.

"No, no," said Scrooge. "I am in earnest. Go and buy it, and tell 'em to bring it here, that I may give them the direction where to take it. Come back with the man, and I'll give you a shilling. Come back with him in less than five minutes, and I'll give you half-a-crown!"

The boy was off like a shot. He must have had a steady hand at a trigger who could have got a shot off half so fast.

"I'll send it to Bob Cratchit's!" whispered Scrooge, rubbing his hands, and splitting with a laugh. "He shan't know who sends it. It's twice the size of Tiny Tim. Joe Miller never made such a joke as sending it to Bob's will be!"

The hand in which he wrote the address was not a steady one, but write he did, somehow, and went downstairs to open the street door, ready for the coming of the poulterer's man. As he stood there, waiting his arrival, the knocker caught his eye.

"I shall love it, as long as I live!" cried Scrooge, patting it with his hand. "I scarcely ever looked at it before. What an honest expression it has in its face! It's a wonderful knocker! – Here's the Turkey. Hallo! Whoop! How are you! Merry Christmas!"

It *was* a Turkey! He never could have stood upon his legs, that bird. He would have snapped 'em short off in a minute, like sticks of sealing-wax.

"Why, it's impossible to carry that to Camden Town," said Scrooge. "You must have a cab."

The chuckle with which he said this, and the chuckle with which he paid for the Turkey, and the chuckle with which he paid for the cab, and the chuckle with which he recompensed the boy, were only to be exceeded by the chuckle with which he sat down breathless in his chair again, and chuckled till he cried.

Shaving was not an easy task, for his hand continued to shake very much; and shaving requires attention, even when you don't dance while you are at it. But if he had cut the end of his nose off, he would have put a piece of sticking-plaster over it, and been quite satisfied.

He dressed himself "all in his best", and at last got out into the streets. The people were by this time pouring forth, as he had seen them with the Ghost of Christmas Present; and walking with his hands behind him, Scrooge regarded every one with a delighted smile. He looked so irresistibly pleasant, in a word, that three or four good-humoured fellows said, "Good morning, sir! A merry Christmas to you!" And Scrooge said often afterwards, that of all the blithe sounds he had ever heard, those were the blithest in his ears.

He had not gone far, when coming on towards him he beheld the portly gentleman, who had walked into his counting-house the day before, and said, "Scrooge and Marley's, I believe." It sent a pang across his heart to think how this old gentleman would look upon him when they met; but he knew what path lay straight before him, and he took it.

"My dear sir," said Scrooge, quickening his pace, and taking the old gentleman by both his hands. "How do you do. I hope you succeeded yesterday. It was very kind of you. A merry Christmas to you, sir."

"Mr Scrooge."

"Yes," said Scrooge. "That is my name, and I fear it may not be pleasant to you. Allow me to ask your pardon. And will you have the goodness" – here Scrooge whispered in his ear.

"Lord bless me," cried the gentleman, as if his breath were taken away. "My dear Mr Scrooge, are you serious?"

"If you please," said Scrooge. "Not a farthing less. A great many back-payments are included in it, I assure you. Will you do me that favour?"

"My dear sir," said the other, shaking hands with him. "I don't know what to say to such munificence."

"Don't say anything, please," retorted Scrooge. "Come and see me. Will you come and see me?"

"I will," cried the old gentleman. And it was clear he meant to do it.

"Thank you," said Scrooge. "I am much obliged to you. I thank you fifty times! Bless you!"

Charles Dickens